Dedicated to all children
and children-at-heart
who are searching for their place
in this world

Ieoh-Ming Pei was born in 1917,
and people call him I.M. Pei,
He's a Chinese-American architect
who would be over 100 years old today!
He won so many awards
and designed so many buildings
that would leave you in a trance,
He most famously designed
the Louvre Pyramid
located in Paris, France.

Over 40 years later, another
Chinese-American architect was born
named Maya Lin,
Winning a contest to design the
Vietnam Veterans Memorial is when her
career would really begin,
People doubted her ideas and skills
because she was just a young student,
But she knew the power of names
would touch the heart of every human.

Umpeleya Marsema Balinton
was known as Sugar Pie DeSanto
in the 1960s,
She had a powerful voice
and did back flips on stage,
making rhythm and blues history,
She grew up with the famous singer
Etta James and had a hit song called,
"I Want to Know,"
Her father was an immigrant from the
Philippines, and her African-American
mother loved to play the piano.

Have you heard of the composer
Robert Lopez who is also part Filipino?
You probably know his famous songs
from the movies "Frozen" and "Coco."
He's the youngest person to ever win an
Emmy, Grammy, Oscar, and Tony award,
He's proud of his Pinoy heritage
and visited the Philippines
where he was adored.

Victoria Ka'iulani was the last princess
of the kingdom of Hawaii,
She was talented in music and art
and grew up with peacocks and
a pony named "Fairy,"
Her name means "the highest point of
heaven" or "royal sacred one,"
She is remembered for fighting for the
independence of her
people, nation, and throne.

Duke Kahanamoku was a Native Hawaiian
known as the Father of Surfing,
He was multi-talented
and worked as a sheriff, an actor,
and even taught hula dancing,
Nicknamed "The Big Kahuna,"
he was a hero who saved the lives
of eight men at sea,
His spirit of Aloha is remembered
with a bronze statue placed in Waikiki.

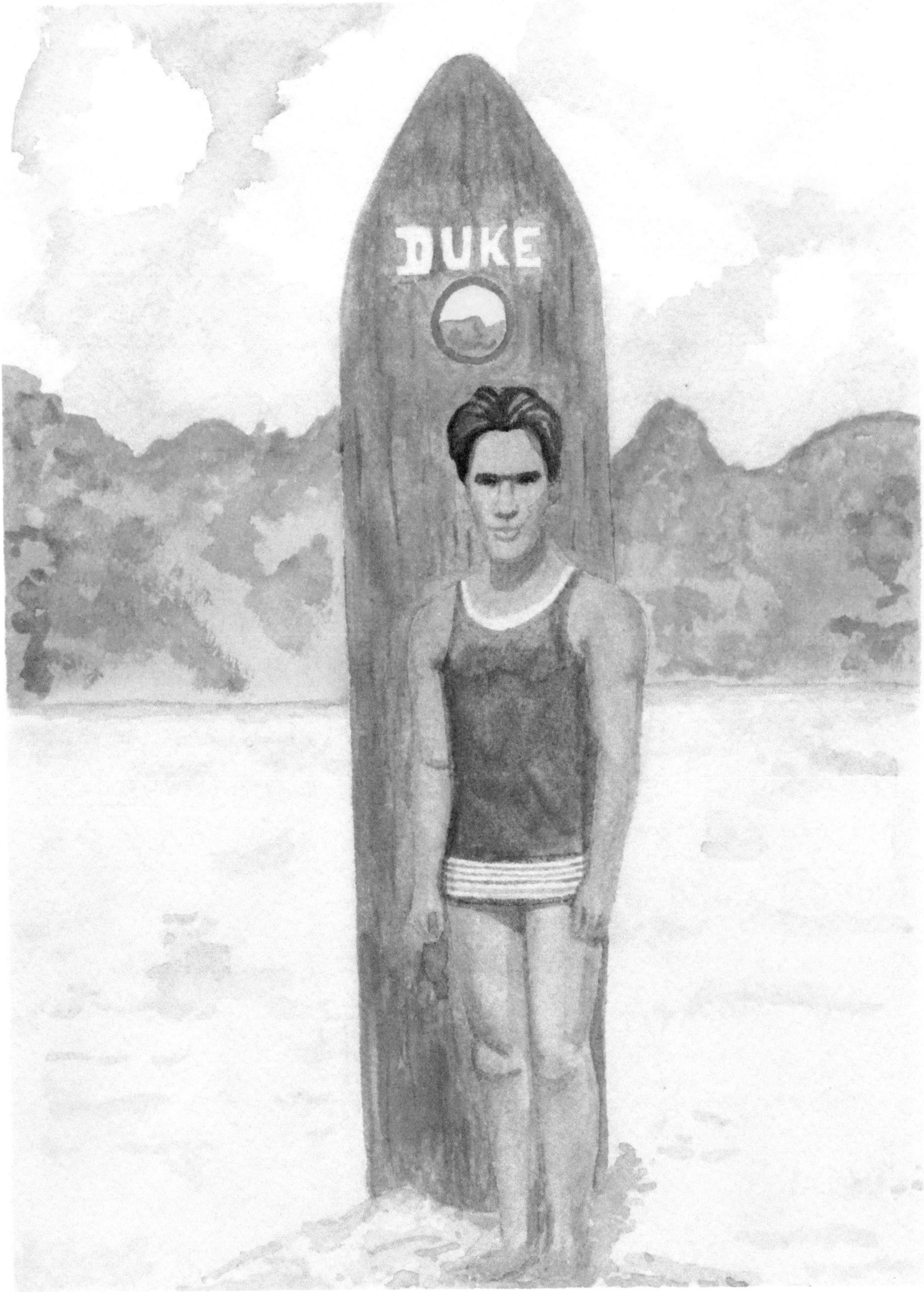
DUKE

Kalpana Chawla was the first
Indian American woman to fly into space,
Since she was a child,
she believed it was important
to have big dreams to chase,
She lost her life on her second mission
and received a
Congressional Space Medal of Honor,
The way she inspires young women and
girls led to streets and buildings
being named after her.

In 1957, Dalip Singh Saud became the first Asian American Congressman, He was born in India and fought for the rights of South Asian immigrants to become U.S. citizens, He was a farmer but also earned a Masters degree and PhD in math, He believed that peace could only be achieved through a non-violent path.

Yuji Ichioka was a historian who first
turned "Asian American" into a word,
It was so all the voices of people whose
families were from Asia could be heard,
During WWII, Yuji was unfairly jailed in a
camp because his parents
were from Japan,
So he made sure history was
recorded correctly so that nothing unfair
like that could ever happen again.

The first woman of color to serve as a
U.S. Congresswoman was
Patsy Takemoto Mink,
She was Japanese American and lived her
life by example to push others to think,
She passed a law that finally allowed girls
to play any sport or activity in school,
She fought for equality and always
pushed against what she thought
were outdated rules.

The first Asian American to ever win
a U.S. Olympic gold medal was
the diver Sammy Lee,
He was only allowed in the
public pool once a week
because of his Korean ancestry,
Some neighborhoods wouldn't allow him to
buy a house, even though he was a
military doctor and an American hero,
But he never let the discrimination
stop him and always strived
for a better tomorrow.

Chloe Kim is the youngest girl to ever win
an Olympic gold medal in snowboarding,
As a 17-year-old Korean American,
she thought representing the U.S. and her
parents' home country was so rewarding,
When she was younger, she was
made fun of for her Asian heritage,
especially her eyes,
She now wants to fight against bullying
and show everyone she's just a normal girl
who loves pizza, churros, and fries.

Truong Tran was born in Vietnam and
moved to the United States
when he was five,
He's an award-winning poet, author, and
artist who most famously made
9,000 paper butterflies!
He loves to make art with items other
people have thrown away,
He's also a college professor who teaches
people to write in creative ways.

Kelly Marie Tran is a
Vietnamese American actress whose
parents were refugees,
She became the first Asian American
woman to have a leading role in a
Star Wars movie,
She believes that all types of faces
and all types of bodies should be
represented on the screen,
As an actress and a writer, she hopes to
redefine the way beauty can be seen.

All these Asian American and
Pacific Islander role models are people
I wish I had learned about
when I was young,
Because rarely seeing any leaders who
looked like me made me feel like
I was all alone,
But I realized my family members were
some of my greatest heroes who always
tried their best and believed in me,
And that I could also become someone to
do something great and make history.

Jasmine Cho was born in Los Angeles, California to parents who immigrated from South Korea. Her lived experience as someone who identifies as Asian American has been uniquely shaped by her time living throughout the country from New Mexico to Hawaii before settling in Pittsburgh, Pennsylvania. Jasmine is the Founder of Yummyholic, an online bakery specializing in custom cookies. Initially using cookie art to explore AAPI issues and matters of representation, she expanded to traditional fine art media while pursuing a degree in Art Therapy at Carlow University.

www.yummyholic.com

CPSIA information can be obtained
at www.ICGtesting.com
Printed in the USA
LVHW071157220919
631864LV00002B/8/P